I0224684

LAST DAYS OF AN OLD DOG

poems by

Patsy Kisner

Finishing Line Press
Georgetown, Kentucky

LAST DAYS OF AN OLD DOG

ACKNOWLEDGMENTS

Grateful acknowledgments to the following journals where these poems first
appeared, some in slightly different versions.

Appalachian Journal: One Still Moment, Sycamore Creek

Cicada: Amid the Melting Snow

Modern Haiku: Purring Louder

Shelia-Na-Gig: Newborn, Shriveled

Tundra: Nearing the Barn

Publisher: Leah Maines

Editor: Christen Kincaid

Cover Art: SteveCrukov/Shutterstock

Author Photo: Patricia Haught

Cover Design: Elizabeth Maines McCleavy

Printed in the USA on acid-free paper.
Order online: www.finishinglinepress.com
        also available on amazon.com

Author inquiries and mail orders:
Finishing Line Press
P. O. Box 1626
Georgetown, Kentucky 40324
U. S. A.

Table of Contents

ONE

Mom's Quilt 1
Remember 2
Newborn 3
Newborn Foal 4
Horse Scent 5
Tag 6
One Still Moment 7
Dog 8
My Gift 9

TWO

Dear Mamaw 13
Old Photos 14
Run 15
What's Gone is Never Gone 16
Potato Digging 17
March 12 18
Thinking of John Muir 19
Pedigree 20
Cup 21

THREE

Yorifumi Yaguchi 25
Touch 26
Last Days of an Old Dog 27
Black Crickets 28
Owl 29
Cheer Up 30
Determination 31
Dawn 32

FOUR

On My Last Day 35
First Date 36
Free 37
Sycamore Creek 38
The Announcement 39

The Farm..40
The Stray...41
The Depression 42
The Sewing Box 43

FIVE

Heaven 47
Colic in the Barn...48
Shriveled 49
Two Fawns...50
Words..51
She Slipped Away...52
Nearing the Barn 53
Amid the Melting Snow...54
Purring Louder 55

SIX

Birth 59
The Difference...60
Dissection..61
Anniversary...62
The Last Night...63
A Universe for Me 64
For the Little Twins 65
After Your Death 66
Today...67

For Phil,
who encourages all things

ONE

MOM'S QUILT

She made it
when a girl
to learn to sew—
odd colors,
not the best cloth,
yet I kept it in a chest,
treasured.
But this morning
I sprung the lock.
As I age I want her quilt
to warm me when
I read
and if, after years,
I've worn every thread
that will be ok.
Love is in the wearing—
what no moth
can eat away.

REMEMBER

when we rode
the horses
through the tall
meadow grass—
they startled
and we held tight
while a dozen
young turkeys
rose
and took flight,
wings flapping low
around us,
you, me and the horses
the center
of a wheel.

NEWBORN

Maria

The first glance
a rush
filled every cell.
Tips of fingers
surged
as well as toes.
The heart ruptured
from the fullness,
but joy healed
it a hundred times,
and that
was only
the beginning.

NEWBORN FOAL

This morning she lies
wet and slick,
a cherry in her eye,
but by noon she
fumbles to find
milk. In the veil
of dusk she jogs
in clumsy circles,
a second hand
to the clock
of her mother—
ticking faster
as she runs
into the night.

HORSE SCENT

It reaches you
before you reach
the barn—
an elaboration
of sweat combined
with moldering earth,
not bitter sour,
but sweet.

TAG

At the creek's
edge
I tag my toes
to water,
and with one
cold shudder
up my spine,
I become
It.

ONE STILL MOMENT

The edge
of the field,
where the willow
droops,
a fawn is
curled in rest.
As I approach
her head
lifts,
and when our
eyes meet
there is
one still moment
before leaving
each other
in peace.

DOG

How I love
to stroke warm fur,
feel you rest
against me,
watch your sides lift
with each soothing breath.

MY GIFT

It's what
I have to give—
I reach a hand
into my heart
and when I raise
it up to open,
birds fly out.

TWO

DEAR MAMAW

In Heaven
will you take
my hand—
let me join you
as we braid
into eternity
the looming
intersections
of at least
a thousand names.

OLD PHOTOS

Faces emerge
that I
have not seen,
and yet soon
we'll hold
each other's
hands.

RUN

back to where
you are loved,
you fool.
Knock down
the door
even though
they'd let you
in. Let them know
you mean it.

WHAT'S GONE IS NEVER GONE

Yesterday
flood waters
boiled,
blistered dreams
to splinters,
but today,
beneath a bulging sun,
an ant goes by
carrying a piece.

POTATO DIGGING

There are times
to fill
buckets,
carry them
by the bails,
feel their weight
stretch muscles,
empty,
then fill
again.

MARCH 12

Last week ten
inches of snow
glistened
beneath the full moon.
Today,
at sixty degrees,
the sun shines,
doves coo,
and the grass
is greener.

THINKING OF JOHN MUIR

I plunge
the well
but I am
dry.
I must run
to the mountains.

PEDIGREE

It came
from the Welsh,
this love
of slopes—
chains
of Appalachian Mountains
coiling around genes
that help us
to remember.

CUP

I cup my hands
to gather words
that only trembling
lips can speak.

THREE

YORIFUMI YAGUCHI

The best inspiration
came from your Japanese
mind. I absorbed it
with the gaping mouth
of a baby bird,
here in the nest
of Appalachia.

TOUCH

On the hand,
the small of a back,
the top of a shoulder,
the soles of feet—
how we know
we are one.

LAST DAYS OF AN OLD DOG

You lie dying,
yet you breathe—
ribs rise then settle
while a whisper
of air floats
above your lips.
I watch, hold
my breath to yours,
exhale and release.

BLACK CRICKETS

always find
their way in,
in they find
their way,
black crickets
on the clean
kitchen floor.

OWL

At night
you scream
and in my ears
you are bigger
than the night—
wings unfolding
to bear
the weight
of dark,
collapsing
prey to ash.

CHEER UP

the wounded jay.
His eyes search
for the missing call
split from beneath his beak—
whistle and remind him
of his song.

DETERMINATION

I had
no scissors
so I improvised
a knife—
cut the truth
out with
my teeth.
I bleed
in sweet relief.

DAWN

As I walk
the ridge
the beech trees
whisper,
and I listen
to their leaves.

FOUR

ON MY LAST DAY

I want to sit
on the sill of the barn,
let the cat rub ankles,
and breathe the horses' breaths.
The family will come
and we'll sort
and restack the hay,
rake out the alley,
then build a fire
in the ring.
The smoke will rise,
and I will too.
Afterwards the cat
will sleep in the loft,
the horses will graze
in the cool of the dark,
the family will rest
in their beds beneath
the tin, and all will be
well, all will be well.

FIRST DATE

In this photo
you are laughing
at the lens,
shy light
in your eyes,
the words
I love you
waiting upon
your lips.

FREE

Untouched by all
that shatters
I glide—
smooth as if
lifted by ice
with warmth
the only telling.

SYCAMORE CREEK

I hear the bullfrog's
throaty bellow
then you are here,
dipping delicate hands
into water to catch
what moves,
while I rest
inside the cusp
of memory.

THE ANNOUNCEMENT

Delight has come
and rests like the fawn
asleep in the weeds.

THE FARM

Planted in the garden,
hoed away weeds,
checked on horses
cooling in the barn,
baking now a cobbler
for supper on the farm.

THE STRAY

Here comes that
stray cat,
now what will
you do—
you feed it,
and it starts
to live
with you.

THE DEPRESSION

Dad

As a boy
you hoed
the neighbors'
fields of corn,
fought sweat bees,
blisters, baking sun
until,
at the end
of all those
green rows,
the man
that had grown
in you
stepped out,
took his wages,
and bought
his mother
a dresser.

THE SEWING BOX

Mom

The sewing box
holds needles,
lace, measuring
tape,
wooden spools
of thread,
and you, of
course, sitting
in your chair
mending us back
together.

FIVE

HEAVEN

came down
on summoning hooves
as the horses
raced across
the pasture.
I watched
along the edge
then followed
after.

COLIC IN THE BARN

Waves of grief
permeate, shake
every rain soaked board
while eyes search
mine for answers—
I can only
look back.

SHRIVELED

I saw you
but you
didn't know me.
Shriveled,
you had fallen
inside yourself
and I was
just a wind.

TWO FAWNS

run behind their mother,
strengthen new legs
that stretch
toward today.

WORDS

sit for a time,
ferment, mutate,
sprout legs
from odd directions
then move.

SHE SLIPPED AWAY

down some crack
in time.
They tried to retrieve her,
but her smile
was too wide.

NEARING THE BARN

the mare stumbles—
her own tracks frozen in mud.

AMID THE MELTING SNOW

the rhododendrons once again
shine green.

PURRING LOUDER

than the others—
the one-eyed cat.

SIX

BIRTH

awaits
inside a mother's womb—
existence floating real
amidst a catacomb.

THE DIFFERENCE

What can cling
onto a breath—
the difference
is life
and death.

DISSECTION

If this thing has guts,
well then let's see them—
pull back the skin,
rip apart the muscle,
gag from the odor,
quiver at the touch.
I could cry from the sight
let alone the taste,
but drinking it down
in one hard swallow
will help me to accept.

ANNIVERSARY

If I could
think back
to all that time
has wrought,
I would still
stand humbled
by what a second
can bring—
the one where
a gaze caught
the glimpse
of another.

THE LAST NIGHT

In the crescent
of last night's
moon I saw
your hand
and thought
the curvature
of the bowl
would keep it
fixed, but
in my sleep
I felt
a touch.

A UNIVERSE FOR ME

Mary

Your sweet voice
still sings
on a distant
wave—within
a universe created
just for me.

FOR THE LITTLE TWINS

Horses pass
yet never fade.
They move to other sod,
give company to God.

AFTER YOUR DEATH

I glance
forward and
there you
are.

TODAY

was a gift.
May I give
it back
in song?

Patsy Kisner lives on a farm in Calhoun County, West Virginia. She and her husband, Phillip, are the parents of two daughters, Mary, now deceased, and Maria, who lives with her family nearby.